Know the Game

SSOCIATION FOOTBALL

CONTENTS

Printed in Great Britain by Dixon & Stell Ltd., Cross Hills, Nr. Keighley E3404

Foreword

The first edition of "Know the Game" was published in 1948. The idea of writing about the Laws of the Game and illustrating them with a large number of drawings to emphasise their purpose and official interpretation, immediately appealed to the interest of schoolboys, senior players and spectators. Such was the success of the experiment that a whole series of "Know the Game" books for other games and sports was then published.

This entirely revised edition of the book fulfils the same purpose as its predecessors, that of providing an attractively illustrated guide to the Laws of Association Football which we hope will encourage players and spectators to take an intelligent interest in the technical details of the game.

It must be said that while the laws of a game outline a code of behaviour it is the spirit behind them which is important. A game can be spoiled even though it is played to the letter of the law, for if so minded it is not difficult to find ways and means of taking unfair advantage over an opponent. We, in these islands, have a fine sports tradition for "playing the game" and of keeping to the unwritten spirit of fair play, handed to us from past generations. It is a heritage we should be proud to honour at all times.

A. Stephens

Chairman, F.A. Council.

The Players

A game of football is played between two teams of not more than eleven players, one of each team must be the goalkeeper.

Substitutes, up to a maximum of two per team, are permitted in a friendly match and also, provided that the authority of the International Association or National Associations concerned has been obtained, in a match played under the rules of a competition. Before the start of a match the referee shall be informed of the names of the substitutes up to a maximum of five from whom the two substitutes may be chosen.

One of the other players or a named substitute (if allowed) may change place with the goalkeeper provided that notice is given to the referee before the change is made. If the change is made during the game, at the half time interval, or at any other interval, or during extra time, without the referee being notified and the player or substitute then intentionally handles the ball within his own penalty area, a penalty kick shall be awarded against his side.

If a player enters or re-enters the field of play to join or re-join his team after the game has commenced, or if he leaves the field of play (except through accident or normal movement of play) in either case without the consent of the referee, he shall be cautioned.

Some Leagues have a compulsory ruling that the players must wear numbers on the backs of shirts or jerseys.

The diagram shows the approximate positions of the players when a team is kicking off, though during a game they will interchange positions freely.

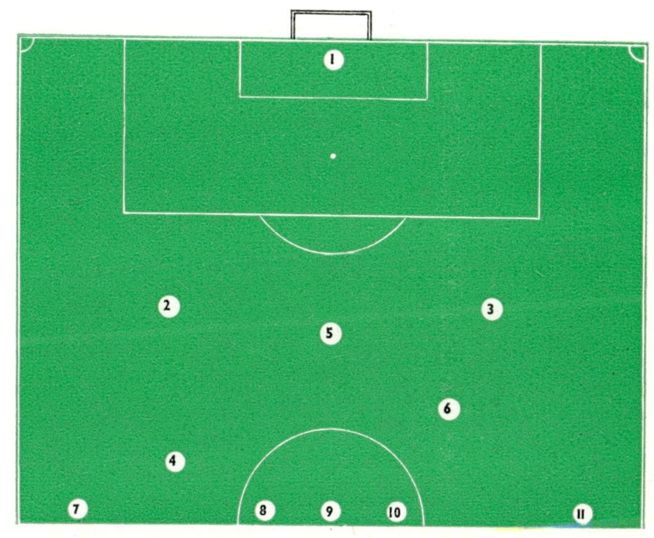

Players' Dress

The usual equipment of a player consists of jersey or shirt, shorts, stockings, shin guards and boots.

A player should not wear anything which may cause injury to another player. He may wear spectacles at his own risk. Colours should be distinguishable as between two opposing sides, with the goalkeeper's jersey distinguishable in colour from those of the other players.

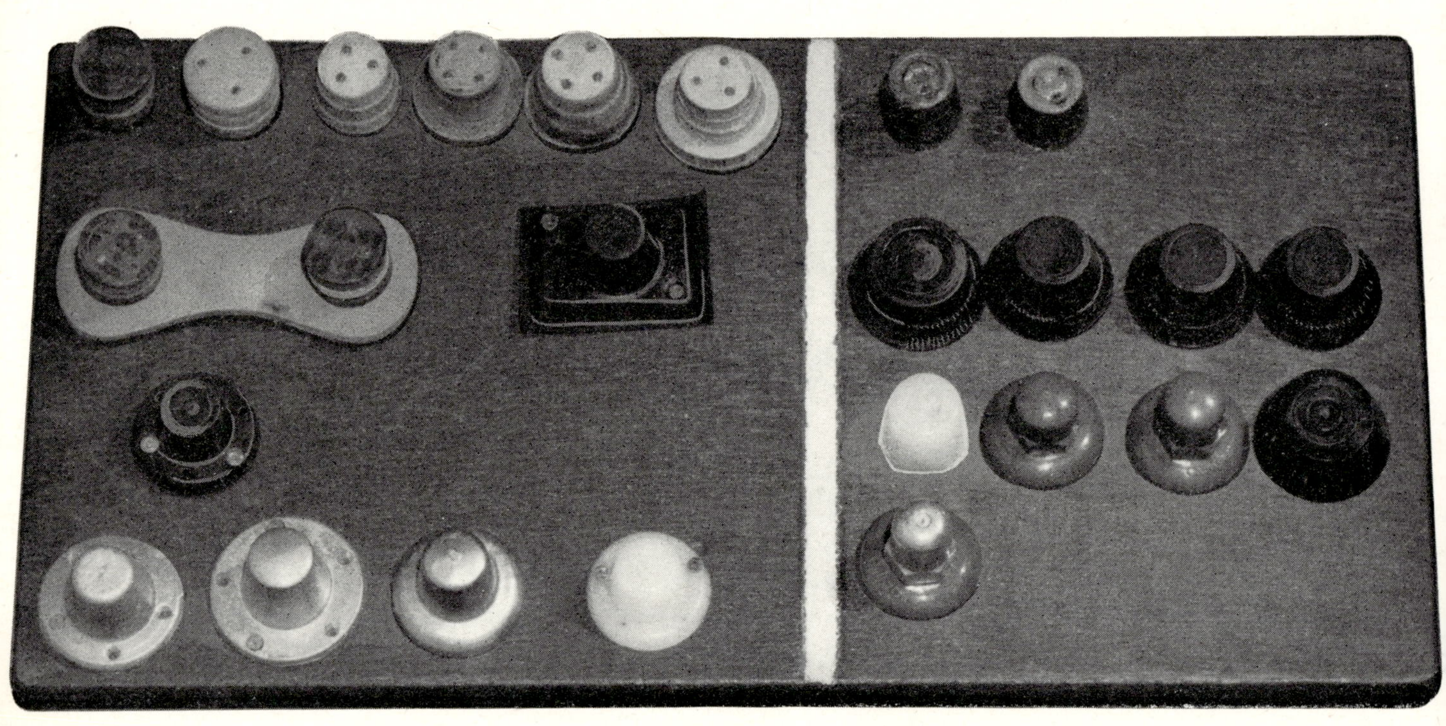

Examples of the types of studs allowed by the Football Association.

If a player is found to have any article of personal equipment not conforming to the foregoing requirements he shall be sent off the field to remedy the fault, and shall not return without first reporting to the referee, who shall satisfy himself that the player's kit is in order. The player shall only enter the field at a moment when the ball has ceased to be in play, and must report to the referee.

Boots

Boots are the most important part of a player's equipment. Much experimenting has been done to produce a boot suited to individual requirements, yet conforming to regulations. The lightweight boot, because of comfort and lightness of touch, is now much preferred to the heavy and more durable type.

Boots must conform to the following regulations:—

All studs must be made of leather, soft rubber, aluminium, plastic or similar material. Bars must be made of leather or rubber. Studs should be round and solid in plan. They can be cylindrical or conical in shape but nowhere less than ½ inch (12·7 mm) diameter. Bars shall be traverse and flat (not less than ½ inch (12·7 mm) wide) extending the width of the boot and being rounded at the corners.

Nails shall be driven in flush with the surface. Bars and studs must not project more than ¾ inch (19·1 mm). Combined studs and bars may be worn.

Other than the small metal seating for the screw-in type of stud no metal plates, even though covered with leather or rubber, shall be worn.

It is important that studs should not be less than ½ inch (12·7 mm) in cross section. Loose and uncovered nails are dangerous, so are roughened edges of well-worn metal or nylon studs.

Whilst a metal seating is required for insertion of the new screw type of stud, it is important that this seating is embedded in the sole.

A quick test of the height of a stud or combined bar and stud can be made by using a sixpence which is ¾ inch diameter.

A player must be held responsible for his boots being correctly studded.

The Ball

The ball shall be spherical and have an outer casing of leather or other material approved by the International Board. Nothing shall be used in its construction that may prove dangerous to players. The ball must be 27 inches — 28 inches (686–711 mm) in circumference and at the start of the game its weight must be from 14–16 ounces (396–453 grammes).

Footballs can now be obtained with a waterproofed surface so that the weight will remain approximately the same throughout a game even on wet and muddy grounds.

A white waterproofed ball can be seen better on dark winter days. The ball can only be changed during the game by the consent of the referee.

The lace type football is now giving way to the valve type. If the ball is laced it is important to draw the opening seams close together and to see that the lacing is flat.

The pressure of the ball shall be equal to 15 lb. per sq. inch (1 kg. per sq. cm.).

For games played by schoolboys on rubble pitches, footballs with protected seams are available, and a size 4 is large enough for juniors.

The Field

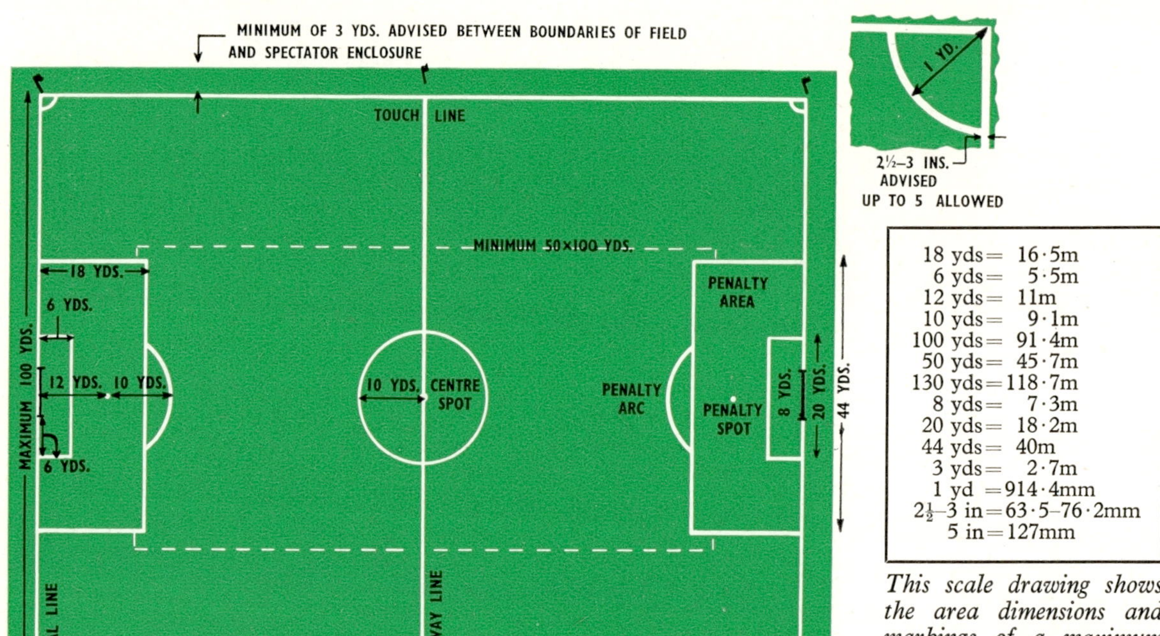

18 yds=	16·5m
6 yds=	5·5m
12 yds=	11m
10 yds=	9·1m
100 yds=	91·4m
50 yds=	45·7m
130 yds=	118·7m
8 yds=	7·3m
20 yds=	18·2m
44 yds=	40m
3 yds=	2·7m
1 yd =	914·4mm
2½–3 in=	63·5–76·2mm
5 in=	127mm

This scale drawing shows the area dimensions and markings of a maximum sized playing field. The dotted line indicates minimum area allowed.

The size of the playing field may have an important bearing on play. Because of difficulty in obtaining adequate playing spaces the laws of the game allow limited variation in dimensions, but stipulate that the length must always exceed the width. Internal markings are however always constant. Clubs should try to obtain a field which conforms to the average dimensions for international matches, i.e., 110 to 120 yards (100–110 metres) by 70 to 80 yards (64–75 metres). It is in the best interests of the game to secure and maintain by effective draining and careful upkeep, a good level field of grass.

Where there is need for continual daily practice on a pitch it may be advisable to lay down a semi-permanent surface of grit instead of turf.

TOUCH LINES are the lines marking the length boundaries of the field. When the whole of the ball passes out of play over either of these lines a throw-in is taken by a player of the side opposed to that of the player who last touched it.

GOAL LINES are the lines at each end of the field, joining and at right angles to the touch lines. When the whole of the ball passes over the goal line (except between the goal-posts and under the crossbar) either on the ground or in the air, the ball is out of play and the game is restarted by:—

1. A Goal Kick — when the ball has last been played by an attacking player.
2. A Corner Kick — when the ball has last been played by or touched a defending player.

When the whole of the ball has passed over the goal line between the goalposts, and under the crossbar, a goal has been scored, unless otherwise provided by the laws.

Note.—Touch lines and goal lines are part of the field of play just as all markings are part of the area which they enclose.

THE HALFWAY LINE indicates a division of the field into two equal halves for the purpose of:—

1. Kick off — when all the players must remain in their own half of the field until the place kick has been taken.
2. Offside — a player cannot be offside if he is in his own half of the field at the moment the ball is played.

THE TEN YARDS CENTRE CIRCLE and the penalty arc (radius ten yards from the penalty mark), provide practical indications of the law that "for all forms of free kick, whether direct or indirect, the players of the *opposing* side shall be at least ten yards from the ball and shall not approach within ten yards until the kick has been taken". The purpose is clearly to prevent interference with place kicks, corner kicks, indirect and direct free kicks.

Note:—The above rule — ten yards away from the ball — applies to *opposing* players standing behind the ball as well as those in front of it, except in three cases:—

1. For a penalty kick, all players, other than the goal-keeper and the player taking the kick, must be outside the penalty area within the field of play and ten yards from the ball at the time the kick is taken; the goalkeeper must stand on the goal line between the goalposts.
2. At a goal kick when all attacking players must be outside the penalty area.
3. When an indirect free kick is awarded against a side in their own penalty area but less than ten yards from goal, defending players may stand on their own goal line between the goalposts, or otherwise they must be not less than ten yards from the ball.

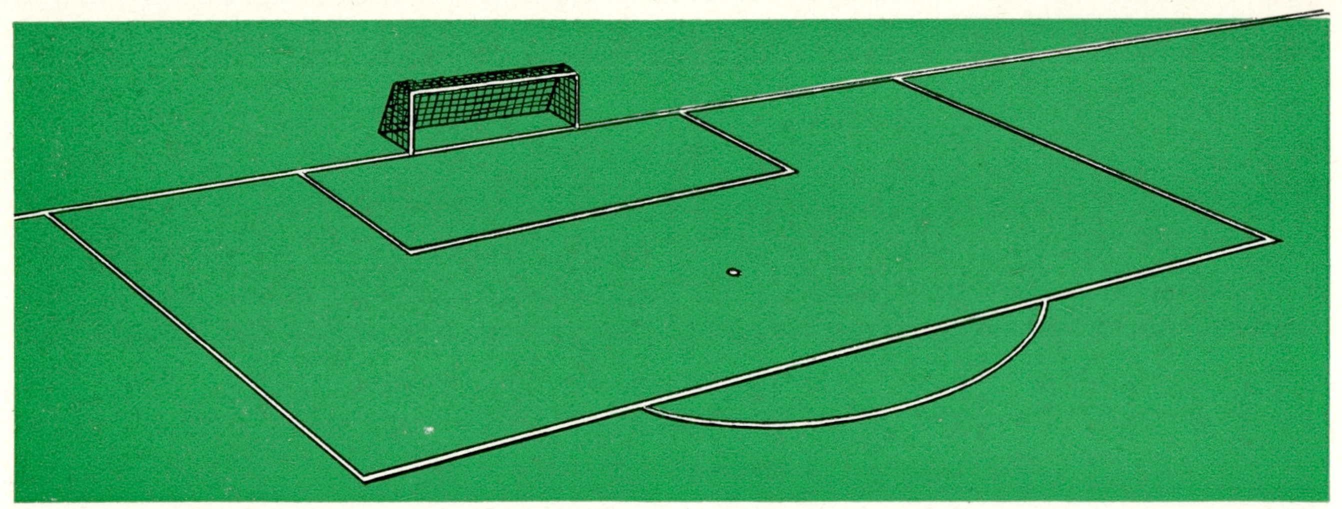

THE PENALTY AREA is a rectangle 44 yards by 18 yards (including the width of line). It serves the following purposes:—

1. Indicates that part of field in which for any of the nine penal offences (see page 22) committed intentionally by a defending player, a penalty kick is awarded.
2. Indicates the part of the field of play where the ball may be handled by the defending goalkeeper.
3. Indicates the area beyond which the ball must be kicked before it is in play from a goal kick or from a free kick awarded to the defending side in their own penalty area.
4. When a penalty kick is awarded, it indicates the area outside which all players, other than goalkeeper and player taking the penalty kick, must stand on the field of play, or outside which all opposing players shall remain while a goal kick or free kick by the defending side is taken.

The penalty arc is not part of the penalty area. By being ten yards from the penalty mark and outside the penalty area, it indicates the additional area into which encroachment is not permitted when a penalty kick is being taken. For a penalty kick, the ball is placed on the penalty mark, approximately nine inches (228·6 mm) in diameter and 12 yards on the field of play from the centre of the goal line.

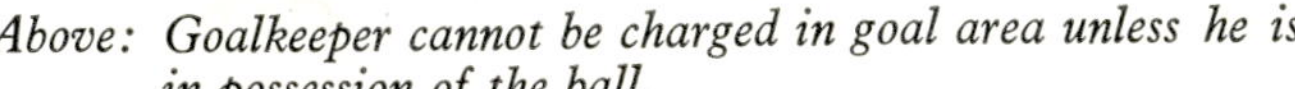

Above: *Goalkeeper cannot be charged in goal area unless he is in possession of the ball.*

Right: *Goalkeeper can be fairly charged outside the goal area.*

THE GOAL AREA has two purposes:—

1. To indicate the area in which the goalkeeper has special protection (can only be charged when in possession of the ball or is obstructing an opponent).
2. To limit area in which ball is placed for a goal kick.

For a goal kick the ball can be placed anywhere in that half of the goal area nearer to where it crossed the goal line.

Many goalkeepers place the ball near the forward corner of the goal area because such position adds a few yards to their kick or allows them a convenient run but most likely because it is the accustomed position. If the ball were placed a little away from the extreme corners it might afford better footing at the time the kick is made.

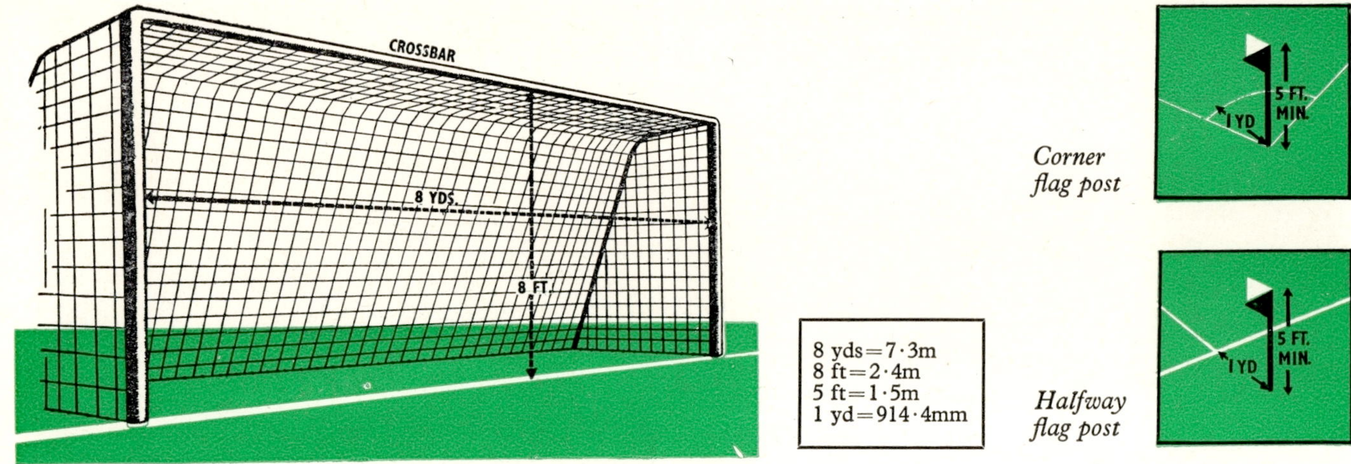

Corner flag post

Halfway flag post

The Goals

Width and depth of goalposts and crossbar must not exceed 5 inches (127 mm). They may be square, rectangular, round, semi-circular or elliptical in shape.

Goalpost and crossbar may only be made of wood or metal. They should be painted white.

Whilst their use is advised, nets are not compulsory except under the rules of certain competitions. Nets, which should be whole, should be properly pegged down, and so fastened to the back of goalposts and bars that they are not hazardous to the goalkeeper. Wire mesh is not permitted since it is dangerous to players.

Flag Posts

Must be firmly fixed, but not too rigid or they may cause injury to a player colliding with them. They may not be removed or inclined to assist a player to take a kick. Corner flag posts must not be less than 5 feet high with a non-pointed top. They mark the corners, and assist the officials in deciding whether the ball passing close to the corner has gone over the touch line or the goal line. Halfway flag post is not essential, but if used, must be opposite the halfway lines and not less than 1 yard outside the touch line.

The Officials

There are three officials responsible for the control of a game of football, an appointed referee, who has primary responsibility and who controls the game on the field of play, and two linesmen one to each touch line.

The referee should have two good whistles, two reliable watches, a coin, a notebook and pencil. Appointed linesmen should each have a watch, a linesman's flag and a whistle (in case of emergency). The flags, which should be of contrasting colour, are usually provided by the home club. Experience has proved that orange-yellow and flame red are good colours for flags. The linesman should always carry his flag unfurled so that his signals will be clearly seen. The laws make no stipulation concerning the dress of the officials, but it is customary to wear kit clearly distinctive from that of the players, particularly in the case of stockings and jacket.

Laws of Play

START OF PLAY

It is customary for the captains of the two teams to shake hands with the referee and each other before the game starts, and then for the home captain to toss a coin, giving the visiting captain the call.

The captain winning the toss may choose — (a) to kick off, or (b) which end of the field his team will defend.

Correct kick off. Players in own half of field and opponents 10 yards from ball. Ball kicked forward to travel more than 27 inches.

Incorrect kick off. Opponents advancing nearer than 10 yards before kick off. Ball kicked backward, kick to be retaken.

If he chooses (a), the other captain has the choice of ends. For the kick-off, the ball is placed in a stationary position on the centre mark. The referee gives the signal for the kick-off and a player of the team kicking off then takes a place kick.

THE KICK OFF

1. Every player must remain in his own half of the field until the ball has been played. Players of the team opposing that which is kicking off must be at least 10 yards from the ball until it is kicked off.
2. The ball must be kicked into the opponents' half of the field.
3. The ball must travel the distance of its circumference to be in play.
4. The kicker must not play the ball a second time until it has touched or been played by another player.
5. For infringements of the law concerning the start of play, the place kick (kick off) shall be retaken. Where, however, the kicker plays the ball a second time as in (4), the game having otherwise correctly started, an indirect free kick shall be awarded to the opposing side.
6. A goal cannot be scored direct from a place kick (kick off).

When a goal is scored the game is restarted in a like manner by the team losing the goal.

After half time ends are changed and the game restarted by the opposite team to that which started the game.

When extra time is necessary, the captains again toss for kick-off or choice of ends.

DURATION OF THE GAME

The game is divided into two equal periods, each of 45 minutes duration, unless, subject to competition rules, reduced equal periods are mutually agreed upon before the game begins. The half-time period of 5 minutes shall not be exceeded except by the consent of the referee.

In certain competitions the rules specify the time to be played and also extra time which may be necessary in the case of a drawn game. The interval between the end of the normal period of play and the start of the extra period shall be under the jurisdiction of the referee. The duration of such interval shall be at the referee's discretion. Referee and players must abide by these rules and regulations.
In all games a referee is empowered to:—

1. Make allowances in either half of the game for time lost through accident or other cause. The amount of time added to make up for time lost is a matter for the discretion of the referee.

2. Extend time to permit a penalty kick to be properly taken at or after the expiration of the normal period of time in either half of the game or in extra time.

SUSPENSION OF PLAY

If play is stopped for an infringement of the laws, the game is restarted by an appropriate free kick.

In certain cases play may be suspended for a cause not specifically mentioned in the laws.

Provided the ball has not passed out of play immediately prior to the suspension, the referee restarts the game by dropping the ball at the place where it was when play was suspended.

The ball is in play when it touches the ground.

If a player touches the ball before it reaches the ground it must be re-dropped. The laws do not stipulate that players should be around the ball when it is dropped.

Examples where a game is restarted by dropping the ball:—

1. After play has been suspended because of injury to player or official.

2. When the ball becomes lodged between two players and the situation may cause injury.

3. Interference by spectators causing the game to be stopped.

4. When the ball bursts, etc.

Should the ball have passed out of play immediately prior to suspension, the game is restarted by the appropriate method—i.e., goal kick, throw in, etc.

Players and officials should keep the time lost through stoppages to a minimum.

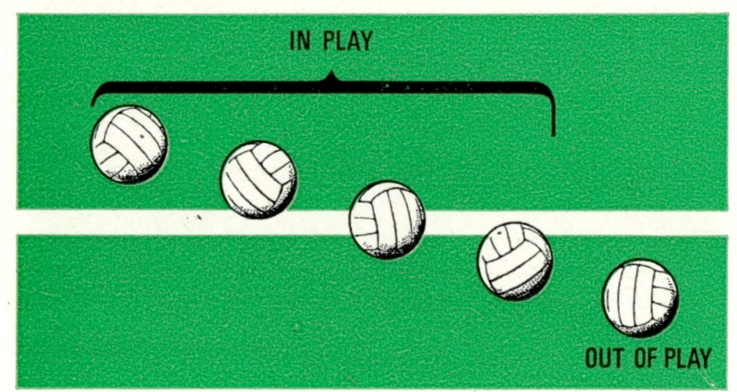

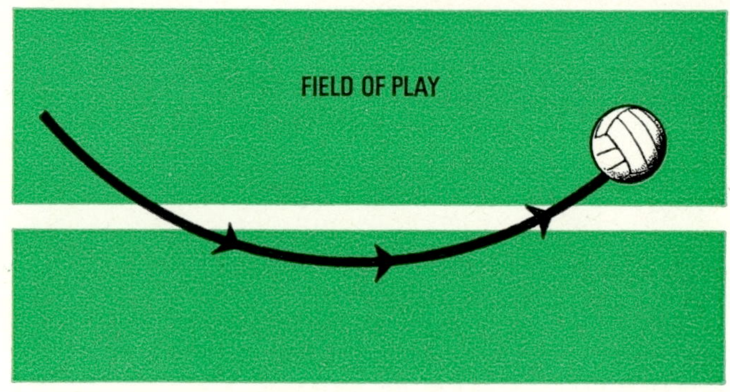

1. A ball may pass out of play during its flight, but swerve or be blown so that it falls in the field of play. It should be given out of play.

BALL IN AND OUT OF PLAY

The markings on the ground are within the field of play, the outer edge being the true boundary line. The ball is out of play only when it has wholly crossed the goal or touch line in the air or on the ground.

The ball is not out of play when it rebounds off referee or linesman when they are on the field of play nor if the ball rebounds off goalpost, crossbar or corner flag into the field of play.

2. Ball strikes referee from throw-in — play on.

The Ball is out of play

3. It is possible for the ball to be out of play when a player plays it or goalkeeper catches it, even though he is standing in the playing area.

The Ball is in play.

4. A player running outside the playing area may still keep the ball in play.

The Ball is in the Penalty Area.

5. A goalkeeper having come out of the penalty area dives to handle the ball. Though part of his body is on the ground outside the area, the ball is clearly in the penalty area when handled. It is the position of the ball which counts.

THE THROW-IN

When the ball goes out of play by passing wholly over the touchline, either on the ground or in the air, it shall be "thrown in" **from the point where it crossed the line.** The following points relate to the throw-in:—

1. The throw-in is taken by an opponent of the player who last played or was touched by the ball before it went out of play.
2. At the moment of delivering the ball the thrower must face the field of play.
3. At the moment of delivering the ball part of each foot must be on the ground either on the touch line or on the ground outside the touch line.
4. The thrower must use both hands.
5. The thrower must deliver the ball from behind and over his head.
6. The ball is in play immediately it is thrown and it passes over the touch line.
7. The thrower must not play the ball until it has been touched or played by another player. If he does so, an indirect free kick is taken by an opponent, from the place where the infringement occurred.
8. A goal cannot be scored direct from a throw-in.
9. If the ball is improperly thrown in, the throw-in is taken by a player of the opposing team.
10. A player cannot be offside direct from a throw-in.

Ball must be behind and over the head

The whole ball must be behind the head at the start of the throw and be thrown over the head. Players should make certain that there is no doubt by taking the ball well over and behind the head, before throwing in.

It is sometimes wrongly assumed that the player must release the ball whilst his hands are over his head. In a natural throwing movement, the hands will always be in front of the vertical plane of the body when the ball is released. The throw *starts* from behind the head and there should then be a continuous movement to the point of release.

Incorrect

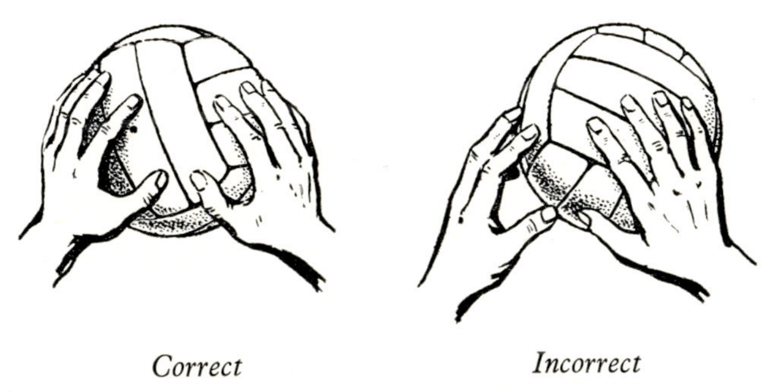

Correct *Incorrect*

Ball must be thrown by both hands

Both hands should be used in throwing the ball. It is wrong to throw in the ball with one hand even though the other is touching or guiding the ball. Make sure the ball goes back *behind* the head.

Part of each foot must be on or outside the touch line

A player may raise his heels or drag his foot in making a throw, but he must have part of each foot on the ground, on or outside the touch line, at the time the throw-in is made. Players who have one or both feet on the line when throwing may, by raising their heels, have the part of the foot touching the ground in the field of play and not on the line, which is infringing the law.

Unless the ball passes across the touch line into the field of play direct from the throw-in, it must be re-thrown correctly.

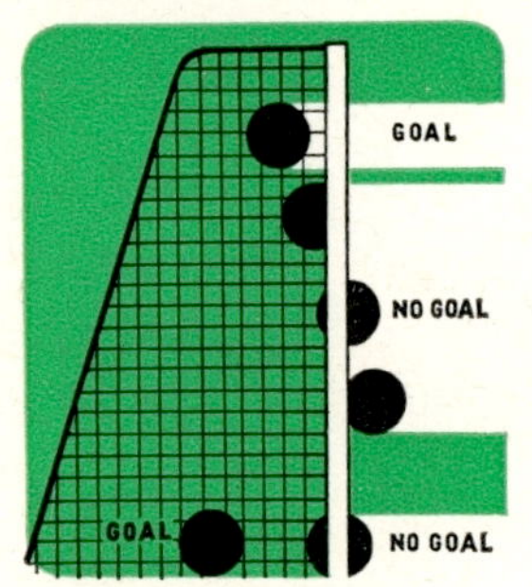

SCORING A GOAL

1. The whole of the ball must pass over the whole of the goal line between the posts and under the crossbar.
2. The ball must not be thrown, carried, or propelled by hand or arm of a player of the attacking side except in the case of the goalkeeper from his own penalty area.
3. If the crossbar has been momentarily displaced, the referee must judge whether the ball has passed the goal line between the posts and below where the crossbar should be, and in such a case allow a goal.

In factor (2) only the attacking side is mentioned, thus if a defending player handles the ball, should it pass over the line into the goal, a goal is scored. Should a goal be prevented by a defending player, other than the goalkeeper, handling the ball a direct free kick is awarded to the attacking side — or if the offence occurred in the penalty area a penalty kick is awarded.

Although conditions (1) and (2) are fulfilled, a goal cannot be scored from an indirect free kick unless the ball has been kicked or touched by a second player, i.e., attacker or defender other than the kicker, before passing through the goal.

If an attacker taking an indirect free kick, kicks directly into his opponents' goal, a goal kick is awarded to the defending team.

If a defender taking an indirect free kick from outside his penalty area, kicks into his own goal, a corner kick is awarded to the attacking team. Similarly with a direct free kick, for such kicks can only score direct against the offending side.

GOAL KICK

A goal kick must be taken by a player of the defending team from within the half of the goal area corresponding to the side of the field in which the ball passed over the goal line (including the crossbar).

The ball is not in play until it has passed beyond the limit of the penalty area. Should it not be kicked directly beyond the limit the kick is retaken. Players of the opposing side must remain outside the penalty area whilst the kick is taken. Should any player other than the kicker contact the ball inside the penalty area the kick is retaken.

A goalkeeper shall not receive the ball into his hands direct from a goal kick in order that he may thereafter kick it into play.

When the ball has passed outside the penalty area, the kicker may not play the ball a second time before it has touched or been played by another player. Should he do so an indirect free kick is awarded to the opponents at the place where the infringement occurred.

A goal may not be scored direct from a goal kick.

Opposing players must remain outside the penalty area whilst the kick is being taken.

To encourage a rapid restart of the game the defender should be allowed to take the kick as soon as possible.

CORNER KICK

A corner kick is awarded to the attacking team when the whole of the ball, having been last played by one of the defending team, passes over the goal line either on the ground or in the air, except when it passes into the goal.

The corner kick is taken by a player of the attacking team, within the quarter circle at the corner flag post nearest to the place where the ball passed over the line.

The corner flag post must not be moved whilst the kick is being taken.

A goal may be scored direct from a corner kick.

Players of the opposing team shall not approach within ten yards of the ball until it is in play, i.e., travelled the distance of its circumference.

The player taking the corner kick must not play the ball a second time until it has been played or touched by another player. Should he do so an indirect free kick shall be taken by a player of the opposing team from the place where the infringement occurred.

Normal positions for referee, one linesman and players for corner kick.

FREE KICKS

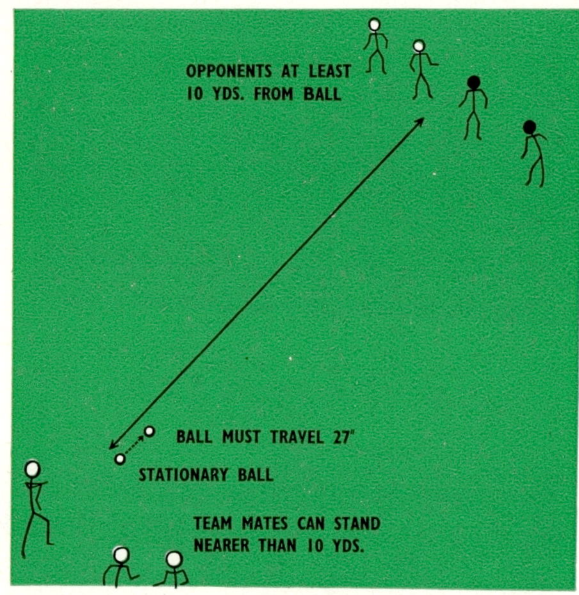

Free kick

Indirect Free Kick

There are two types of Free Kick:—

1. Indirect: from which a goal cannot be scored without the ball touching or being played by another player.
2. Direct: from which a goal can be scored direct against the offending side.

Direct free kicks are awarded for the nine intentional offences listed on page 22.

A penalty kick is awarded if any one of these offences is committed intentionally by a player in his own penalty area.

Free kick from inside own penalty area. All opposing players remain outside the area and must be at least ten yards from the ball whilst the kick is being taken. The ball is considered to be in play immediately it has travelled the distance of its own circumference and is beyond the penalty area. The goalkeeper must not receive the ball into his hands so that he can kick it into play. If the ball is not kicked direct into play beyond the penalty area the kick is retaken.

Free kick outside own penalty area. All opposing players must be at least ten yards from the ball until it is in play. The ball shall be considered to be in play when it has travelled the distance of its own circumference.

The ball must be stationary when a free kick is taken.

If the kicker after taking the free kick, plays the ball a second time before it has been touched or played by another player an indirect free kick shall be taken by a player of the opposing team from the spot where the infringement occurred.

THE PENALTY KICK

The Penalty Kick can only be awarded for any of the nine offences (see page 22) intentionally committed by a player of the defending side, within his own penalty area.

If necessary time of play shall be extended at half-time or full-time or in extra time to allow the penalty kick to be properly taken.

The penalty kick is taken from the penalty mark, 12 yards from the mid-point of the goal line.

When the penalty kick is being taken all players other than the goalkeeper and the player taking the kick must be:—

1. On the field of play. 2. Outside the penalty area. 3. At least 10 yards from the ball until the kick has been taken.

Note.—Players may stand along the side lines of the penalty area if they so wish and thus they may also be in front of the ball.

The goalkeeper must stand (without moving his feet) on his goal line between the goalposts until the ball has been kicked by the player taking the penalty kick.

The player taking the kick must kick the ball forward, and shall not play the ball a second time until it has been touched or played by another player.

The ball is in play directly it is kicked, i.e., travelled the distance of its circumference.

A goal may be scored direct from such a kick.

If the ball touches the goalkeeper before passing between the posts, even though it is after expiration of half-time or full-time, the goal counts, but if the goalkeeper parries the ball or it rebounds from the woodwork, time must be signalled immediately.

For any infringement by the defending team of the above laws:— if a goal is scored — goal is allowed; if a goal has not been scored — kick retaken.

For any infringement by the attacking team other than the player taking the kick, if a goal is scored it shall be disallowed and the kick retaken.

For any infringement by the player taking the kick, commited after the ball is in play e.g., playing the ball a second time without it having touched or been played by another player, an opponent shall take an indirect free kick from the place where the infringement occurred.

Fouls and Misconduct

Players do not commence a game with intention to foul an opponent or behave in a manner which can be termed misconduct against the principle of fair play. Nevertheless, the referee must be prepared to deal with infringements.

If neglected, fouls may result in retaliation which would ultimately spoil the game.

A player shall be sent off the field if he is guilty of violent conduct or serious foul play, if he uses foul or abusive language, or if he persists in misconduct after receiving a caution.

THE NINE DIRECT FREE KICK OFFENCES

Of these nine offences, all of which have to be intentionally committed, one involves handling the ball intentionally (except in the case of the goalkeeper), whilst the remaining eight are as follows:—

1. Intentionally charging an opponent violently or dangerously.
2. Intentionally charging an opponent from behind (unless the opponent is obstructing).
3. Intentionally holding an opponent.
4. Intentionally pushing an opponent.
5. Intentionally striking or attempting to strike an opponent.
6. Intentionally kicking or attempting to kick an opponent.
7. Intentionally tripping an opponent.
8. Intentionally jumping at an opponent.

Direct free kick

OFFENCES FOR WHICH INDIRECT FREE KICK IS AWARDED

All 9 offences are penalised by the award of a direct free kick to the opposing team unless committed by one of the defending side in his own penalty area, in which case a penalty kick is awarded.

Some offences are penalised by the award of an indirect free kick against the offending side: viz

1. Playing in a manner considered by the Referee to be dangerous, e.g., attempting to kick the ball while held by the goalkeeper.

2. Charging fairly, i.e., with the shoulder, when the ball is not within playing distance of the players concerned and they are definitely not trying to play it.

3. When not playing the ball, intentionally obstructing an opponent, i.e., running between the opponent and the ball, or interposing the body so as to form an obstacle to an opponent.

4. Charging the goalkeeper except when he

   (a) is holding the ball,

   (b) is obstructing an opponent,

   (c) has passed outside his goal area.

5. When playing as goalkeeper

   (a) takes more than four steps whilst holding, bouncing or throwing the ball in the air and catching it again without releasing it so that it is played by another player or

   (b) indulges in tactics which, in the opinion of the referee, are designed merely to hold up the game and thus waste time and so give an unfair advantage to his own team.

Indirect free kick.

Intentional or Accidental?

The law states that a player shall be penalised if he intentionally commits an offence. The referee must decide immediately whether the act was intentional or accidental.

(1)

Examples on the Penalty Kick Law

What is the correct decision in each of the following instances:—

(1) Attacker 1 is taking the kick but before he reaches the ball Attacker 2 runs over the 10 yard arc line.

Answer: 2, an attacking player, is infringing the law. Therefore if 1 scores from the penalty the referee orders it to be retaken; if 1 does not score the kick is not retaken.

(2) Attacker 1 takes the kick, but as it enters goal defender runs into the penalty area.

Answer: A Goal. Defender did not move before ball was kicked. In any case if defender had moved before 1 took the kick and a goal had been scored the goal would be allowed.

(2)

(3)

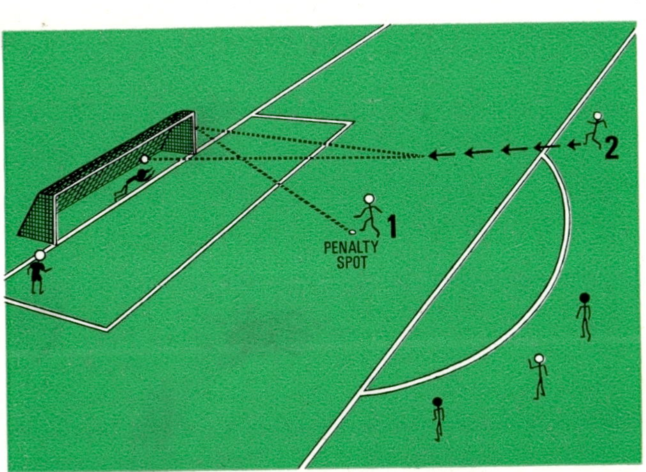

(4)

(3) Attacker 1 kicks the ball which strikes the upright and rebounds to Attacker 2, who runs in and scores.

Answer: A Goal. 2 is not offside and did not move forward into penalty area until 1 had taken the penalty kick. If 1 were in front of 2 when the latter shoots, the referee might adjudge him to be interfering with play and give him offside.

(4) Additional time is being allowed for the penalty kick. Attacker takes the kick which is punched out by the goalkeeper. The same attacker follows up and kicks the ball into goal.

Answer: No Goal. Additional time is allowed for penalty kick only. As the goalkeeper has saved the kick the referee should signal for full-time.

Charge is fair but ball not within playing distance
—indirect free kick

Pushing — use of elbow
—direct free kick

Charge is fair but goalkeeper not in possession
—indirect free kick

CHARGING

Players may charge fairly when the ball is within playing distance of the players concerned and they are definitely attempting to play it, in order either to gain possession of the ball or to retain possession of the ball when challenged by an opponent.

A fair charge is one in which the player fairly "shoulders" his opponent without using his arms as a means of pushing, and which is neither violent nor dangerous, nor from behind.

The law states that the player shall be penalised by a direct free kick against him if he charges in a violent or dangerous manner, or charges an opponent from behind unless the latter is obstructing, and by an indirect free kick if he charges fairly but at the wrong time.

Fair charge—
goalkeeper in possession

Player intentionally obstructing opponent to prevent him reaching the ball —indirect free kick

Fair charge — ball within playing distance

Dangerous play
—indirect free kick

If a player is deliberately obstructing he may be charged, even from behind, providing the charge is not violent or dangerous.

Charging in a dangerous manner should not be confused with dangerous play. The latter is penalised by an indirect free kick.

Dangerous play is generally associated with a player attempting to kick a ball which is sufficiently high for another player to be attempting to head it at the same time. There are other actions which the referee may regard as dangerous and penalise the player for them.

HANDLING

A player has handled the ball if he has intentionally carried, struck or propelled it with his hand or arm.

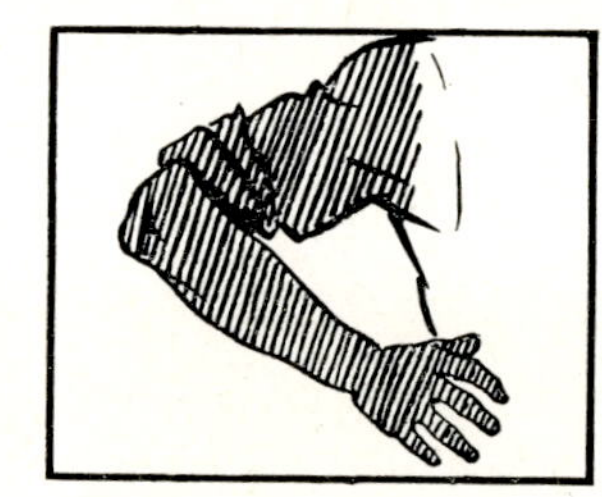

Area covered by "Hands"

It may be impossible for a player to avoid "handling" the ball, having no time to withdraw his hand or arm before the ball strikes him. Even though the player may thus gain advantage, because of the ball being directed along a different path, if it was not intentional the referee should not penalise it. This is vitally important in the penalty area, where a player unable to beat an opponent may deliberately kick the ball directly at him hoping to strike his hand or arm and thus get a penalty.

Intentional—direct free kick

Unintentional

Pushing—direct free kick

Holding—direct free kick

PUSHING AND HOLDING

Body contact in games is likely to cause the use of hands and arms to maintain balance or protect oneself.

A player must in no circumstances use his hands or arms either to hold an opponent back or push him away from the ball. This offence often occurs when the arms of players become interlocked and the referee must be watchful for such infringements which may appear "accidental".

Even though a player is being obstructed intentionally he may not use his hands to push the obstructing opponent away.

Unintentional tripping — Player has tackled for ball and played it cleanly. Opponent late to get possession falls over outstretched leg.

Intentional tripping—direct free kick

Feigned trip

TRIPPING

The referee should be careful to distinguish between an intentional trip and a trip resulting from normal play. It is possible for a player to be tripped or kicked accidentally. In tackling for the ball, for example, it may happen that even though the ball is played the approaching player is tripped unintentionally.

It is also possible for a player to feign a trip in order to gain a free kick even though his opponent does not intentionally trip him.

The referee may decide that a player has not deliberately kicked an opponent, but has been guilty of dangerous play and award an indirect free kick against him.

Jumping for ball

Sliding tackle

Dangerous play—indirect free kick

JUMPING

A player is penalised for jumping at an opponent.

This does not mean that a player commits an offence when, in jumping to head the ball, he makes contact with an opponent.

Jumping for the ball should not be confused with jumping at an opponent. Similarly a player may take a leap to get near the ball without necessarily endangering his opponent.

A sliding tackle done fairly is not dangerous to either player, especially when clear contact is made with the ball, and should therefore not be penalised, but to jump with both feet at the ball in the manner illustrated when it is being played by an opponent can result in injury and is therefore penalised.

1. Player having made a pass to a colleague, intentionally obstructs an opponent to prevent him from tackling player receiving ball.—**Obstruction.**
—indirect free kick

2. Player in possession turning to shield ball from opponent.—**Fair Play.**

OBSTRUCTION

An intentional act to obstruct the path of an opponent to the ball, when not attempting to play the ball oneself, is an offence which is penalised by an indirect free kick. The law describes the offence as:—

"When not playing the ball, intentionally obstructing an opponent, e.g., running between the opponent and the ball, or interposing the body so as to form an obstacle to the opponent."

This offence should not be confused with the type of obstruction which is natural to the game. A player can

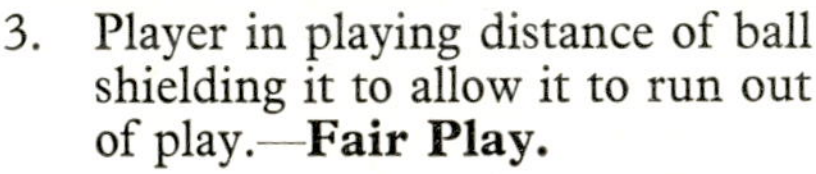

3. Player in playing distance of ball shielding it to allow it to run out of play.—**Fair Play.**

4. Defender having allowed ball to pass him for goalkeeper to field intentionally blocking the path of an attacker.—**Obstruction.**
—indirect free kick

shield the ball with his body when he is playing or attempting to play it. This is a feature of dribbling and close ball control. Obstruction should be distinguished from the personal foul (e.g., pushing, holding) in which case the offence is penalised with a direct free kick (or a penalty kick if committed by a player in his own penalty area).

Finally if an opponent is obstructing a player, the player may charge him providing the charge is not violent or dangerous. Here the referee may use the advantage law by refraining from penalising the obstruction when the player successfully overcomes the obstruction.

5. Player who cannot possibly play the ball (because it is out of distance), intentionally moves with his back to opponent to prevent him from reaching it before it goes out of play.—**Obstruction.**

   —indirect free kick

6. Player having been beaten by the ball reaches out to hold opponent and prevent him from getting possession of it.—**Foul.**

   —direct free kick

7. Player not attempting to play the ball but intentionally blocking the approach of an opponent who is trying to play it.—**Obstruction.**

—indirect free kick

A typical "offside" movement

Offside

In most field games where the main purpose is to score through the opponents' goal, some restrictions are applied to prevent the direct but uninteresting mode of attack, which consists of a player or players waiting in close proximity to the goal, ready to score from short range. The restricting rule in football is known as the offside law, and provides notable technical features of the game. As the punished infringement of this law results in an immediate breakdown of attack, it is essential that the issue of the law should be clearly grasped in all its details.

Stated in full the law says:

"a player is offside if he is nearer his opponents' goal line than the ball at the moment the ball is played:—

Unless:

1. **He is in his own half of the field of play.**
2. **There are two of his opponents nearer to their own goal line than he is.**
3. **The ball last touched an opponent or was last played by him.**
4. **He receives the ball direct from a goal kick, a corner kick, a throw-in, or when it is dropped by the referee."**

A player in an offside position shall not be penalised unless, in the opinion of the referee, he is interfering with the play or with an opponent, or is seeking to gain an advantage by being in an offside position.

For an infringement of the law, an indirect free kick shall be taken by a player of the opposing team from the place where the infringement occurred.

EXAMPLES ON THE OFFSIDE LAW

The above points are illustrated in the following examples.

Player between goal and ball

1. Attacker 1 is about to play the ball. Only his fellow-players in his opponents' half of the field who are nearer than the ball to the goal line are liable to be offside. Dotted line passing through the ball parallel to the goal line marks the division. *2 and 3 cannot be offside at the moment 1 plays the ball, as they were not in front of the ball. But 4 is in an offside position.*

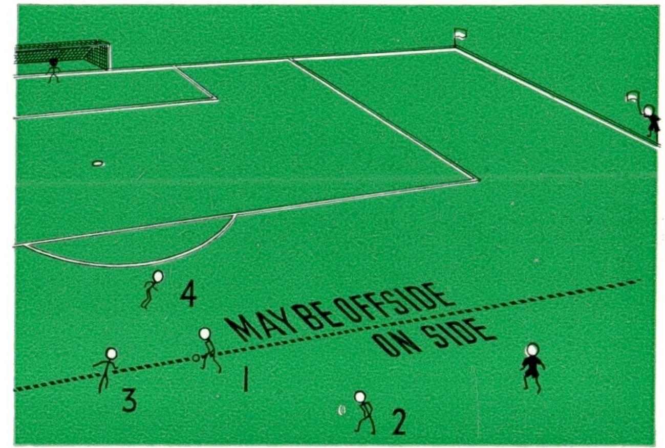

Ball touched by defending player

2. Although Attacker 2 is clearly offside at the moment the ball is played by Attacker 1, and the referee may be about to signal to this effect, if the ball were to touch the defender or be played by him, then 2 may be "Played-onside". If the Referee has signalled before the ball touches or is played by defender then he must allow his decision to stand. One can see the importance here of playing to the referee's signal. A linesman might signal that 2 is in an offside position as soon as 1 plays the ball. On the other hand not having seen the signal, the referee might allow play to continue because the defender has played the ball.

Two defenders nearer goal line

3. Attackers, 2, 3 and 4 are all nearer to their opponents' goal line than the ball. They are in offside **positions.** At the moment No. 1 plays the ball, attackers 3 and 4 **may** become offside (only one opponent between them and defenders' goal line). Attacker 2 is onside (two opponents between him and opponents' goal line).

Interfering with play

4. Attacker 1 passes to Attacker 2. *It might be argued that 3, who is offside, is so far away from the play that he is not interfering. But the defender must have had his attention focused on 3, and therefore the latter is interfering with play indirectly by preventing this defender from being ready to cover 2 in approach to goal.*

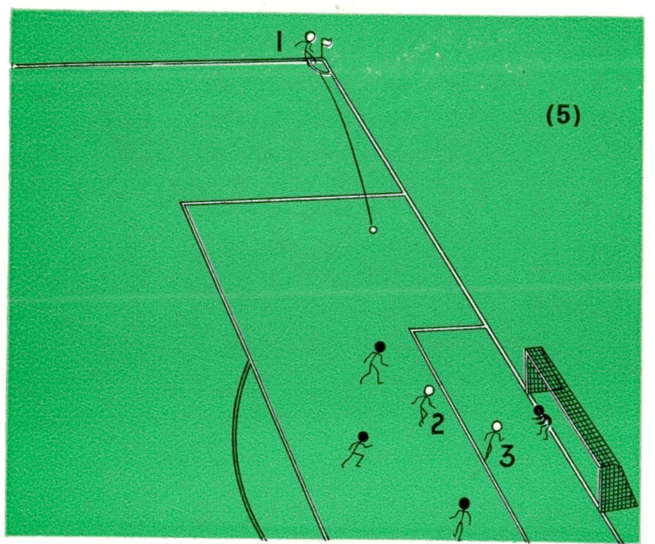

Corner kick, throw-in or when referee drops ball

5. Attackers 2 and 3 cannot be offside from a corner kick, i.e., when the kick is taken. If, however, the ball goes direct from the corner kick to Attacker 2 who then plays it to Attacker 3, the latter is offside. The same principle applies to a throw-in, a goal kick, or when the ball is dropped by the referee.

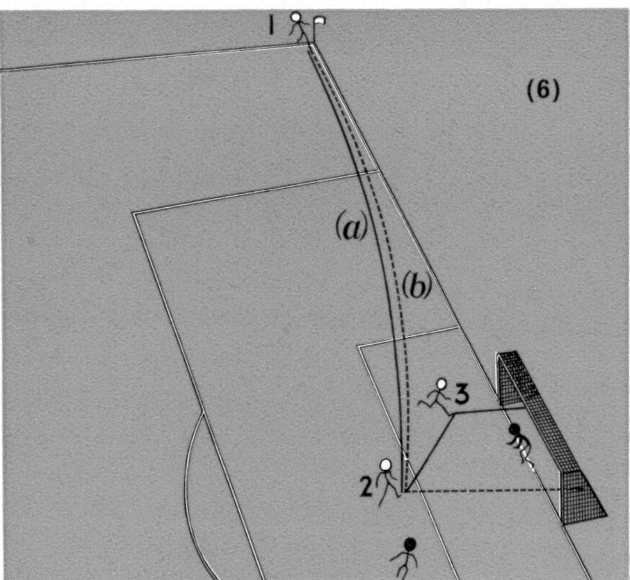

6. (a) Attacker 1 takes a corner which goes to Attacker 2 who shoots but Attacker 3 deflects it into goal. What is the decision?

Answer: Offside — 2 is not offside direct from the corner kick, but 3 is offside when 2 passes the ball to him. 3 is nearer the goal line than the ball and has only one defender, the goalkeeper, nearer to the goal line when the ball is played by 2.

6. (b) Attacker 1 takes a corner which goes to Attacker 2 who shoots and scores without Attacker 3 touching the ball. What is the decision?

Answer: 2 cannot be offside from the corner kick. 3 may be interfering with play in an offside position — therefore goal may be disallowed.

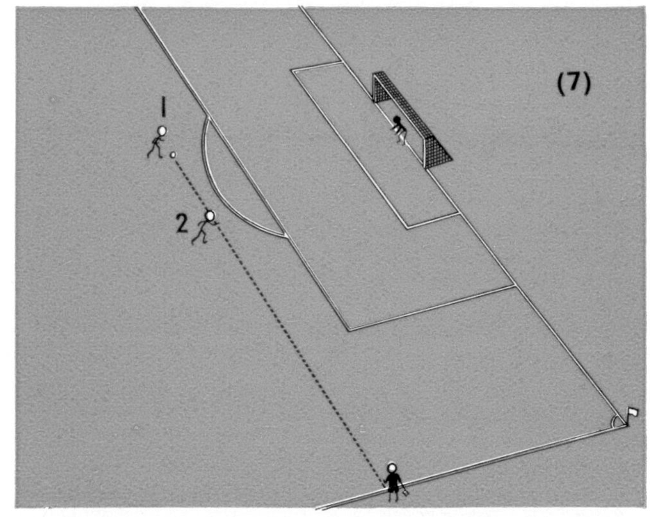

7. Attacker 1, who has beaten the defender, passes to Attacker 2 who scores. What is the decision?

Answer: A Goal. 2 was not offside when 1 played the ball for he was not nearer the goal line than the ball at that moment.

8. (a) Attacker 1 takes a throw-in which goes to Attacker 2 who passes it to Attacker 3 who scores. What is the decision?

Answer: A Goal. 2 is not offside from the throw-in and 3 is not nearer the goal line than the ball when passed by 2.

(b) Attacker 1 takes a throw-in which goes to Attacker 2 who scores directly. What is the decision.

Answer: A Goal. 2 is not offside from the throw-in.

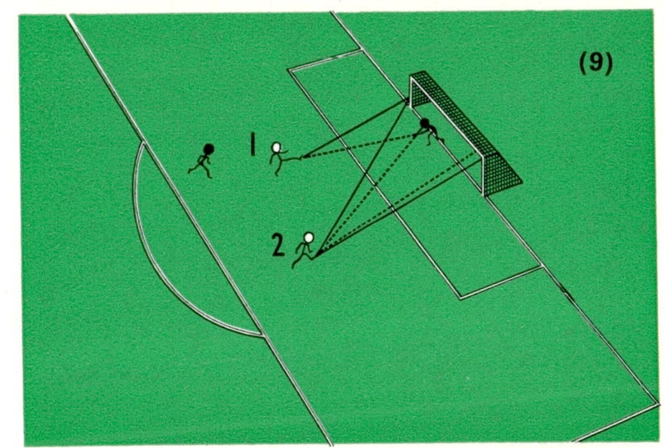

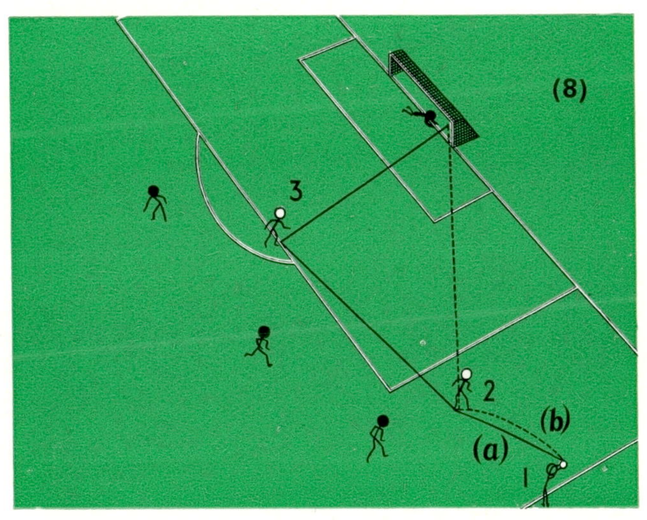

9. (a) Attacker 1, who has dribbled past the defender, shoots but the ball rebounds off the goal post to Attacker 2 who scores. What is the decision?

Answer: 2 is not offside from the rebound since he was not in front of the ball when played by 1. Therefore it is a goal unless the referee adjudges that 1, who is in an offside position, is interfering with play when 2 shoots.

(b) The same circumstances, only this time the goal-keeper fists the ball to Attacker 2 who scores. What is the decision?

Answer: The same as above. 2 is not offside but 1, who is in an offside position when 2 shoots, may be deemed to be interfering with play.

Control of the Game

THE REFEREE

Although he may have two linesmen to assist him, *the referee has the sole responsibility of enforcing the Laws of the Game*. He must know not only the Laws but also their correct interpretation and application.

His decision may well be a matter of opinion. For example he must decide whether a player is tripped intentionally or accidentally; or if a player who is in an offside position is interfering with play. If he decides that an offence has been committed, the referee has to ask himself, "Will stopping play give an advantage to the offending side?"

Uniformity of interpretation of the Laws is one thing — quite a different matter however is the interpretation of the situation to which the Laws have to be applied.

There are specific duties which the referee has to perform. In his enforcement of the Laws he has to:

1. Decide on disputed points.
2. Reject unsuitable match equipment.
3. Allow no unauthorised persons to enter the field of play.
4. Keep a record of the game.
5. Act as timekeeper, allowing for time lost through accident or any other cause.
6. Signal for the stoppage and recommencement of the game.
7. Report the postponement or abandonment of the game.
8. Caution a player guilty of misconduct and send him off if he persists in misconduct.
9. Stop play if he considers a player to be seriously injured.

In addition to a variety of duties. he has discretionary powers. These include stopping the game for an infringement of the laws, suspension or termination of the game for such reasons as adverse weather or ground conditions, or interference by spectators. His power to penalise extends to offences committed when play has been temporarily suspended.

Note:

1. On points of fact connected with play the referee's decision is final as far as the result of the game is concerned.

2. The referee's discretionary powers begin from the time he enters the field of play. His jurisdiction begins from the time he signals for the kick-off.

3. His use of the advantage clause is most important He must ensure that no offending side gains an advantage through being punished.

4. Opponents may seek to delay the taking of a free kick in order to gain an advantage for their team. The referee may therefore allow a quick restart, considering the advantage to the side taking the kick.

5. The referee decides whether or not the ball is to be changed during the game.

6. He is also entitled to compensate for time lost on account of:

   (a) The deliberate wasting of time.

   (b) The treatment of injury on the field of play.

7. He extends time for the taking of a penalty kick.

8. *Cautioning procedure.* The referee should use the following procedure when he cautions a player:

   (a) Tell him that he is to be cautioned.

   (b) Enquire his name.

   (c) Referring to the player by name, plainly state that he is being cautioned and give him the reason for the caution (N.B. the referee must use the word "caution"),

   (d) Plainly state that if he persists in misconduct he will be ordered from the field of play.

Having suspended or abandoned the game, or having cautioned or ordered off a player, the referee must report the matter to the National or Affiliated Association concerned, within two days (Sundays not included). Reports will be deemed to be made when received in the ordinary course of the post.

Referees and linesmen are advised to consult the rules of the competition in which they officiate. The referee in particular needs to be well aware of possible variations regarding appurtenances, the ball, extra time, duration of play, etc.

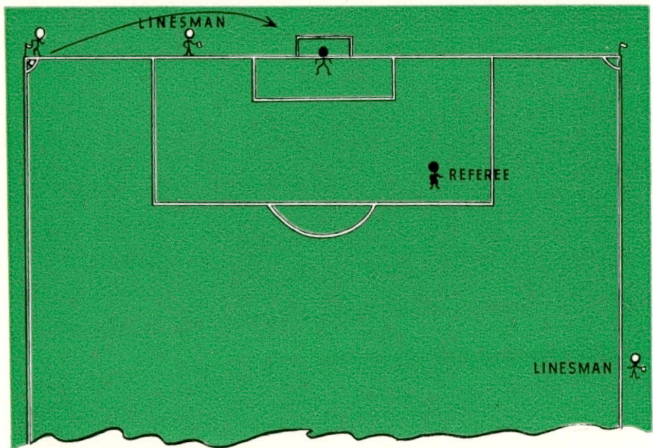

Position of referee and linesmen for corner kick when linesmen are qualified and neutral.

LINESMEN

Two linesmen are required to assist the referee, their duties being to indicate by signal to the referee:—

1. When the ball is out of play.
2. Whether there is a corner kick or goal kick.
3. Which side is entitled to the throw-in.

Linesmen also usually indicate by signal to the referee when a player is "offside" and draw the attention of the referee to rough play, or ungentlemanly conduct. A linesman may also give an opinion on any point on which the referee consults him.

Note:—When a linesman signals to the referee it is not an indication to cease play.

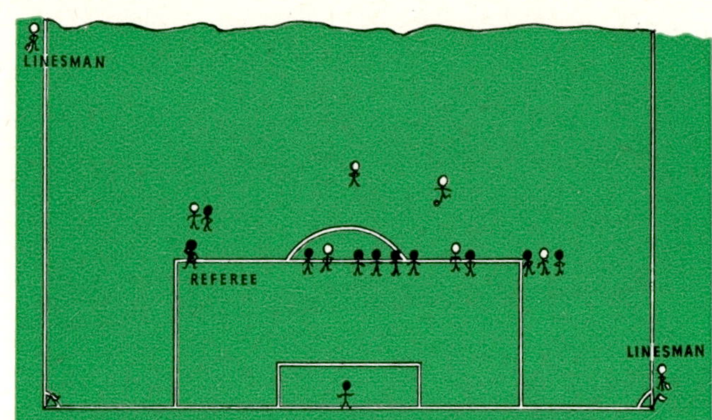

Position of referee and linesmen when free kick being taken.

It is obvious that the full co-operation of linesmen can only be obtained from neutral qualified officials. Some decisions could not be referred to a linesman who was not neutral.

POSITION ON FIELD OF PLAY

A diagonal system of control is advised to obtain the best advantage of covering the whole of the field of play by co-operative effort between the referee and the two linesmen.

The principles involved are:—

(a) The linesmen are suitably positioned to cover each half of the field and therefore to be up with play to judge offside positions.

(b) By diagonal patrol a referee moves so that if play ranges rapidly from wing to wing he is covered by one of the assisting linesmen.

Principle (a). The offside law involves the question of alignment of players, which is only accurately judged by a view of play at right angles to the touch line. Linesmen are better prepared for judging such offences if their patrol is limited to approximately half the touch line.

Principle (b). Whilst the linesman may assist the referee, it is usual for the latter to judge all infringements of play other than ball out of play and offside. If a referee was rigidly adopting the diagonal system, and found himself in position (1) in the diagram when an infringement takes place at (2) he may be too far away to give an accurate assessment, or to, when the atmosphere of play demands, exercise adequate control.

It is better for the referee to keep reasonably close to the play at all times by using a wider diagonal zone, as shown in this diagram. This will still avoid the possibility of having two officials at the same spot and will also allow the referee to move sideways when the position of play demands it.

In many less senior games, the linesmen are not usually neutral, and therefore the referee delegates less responsibility over the game. For such a situation this diagram serves to illustrate the zone of a referee's movements which will keep him in close touch with play and at the same time permit him to move quickly from one area to another.

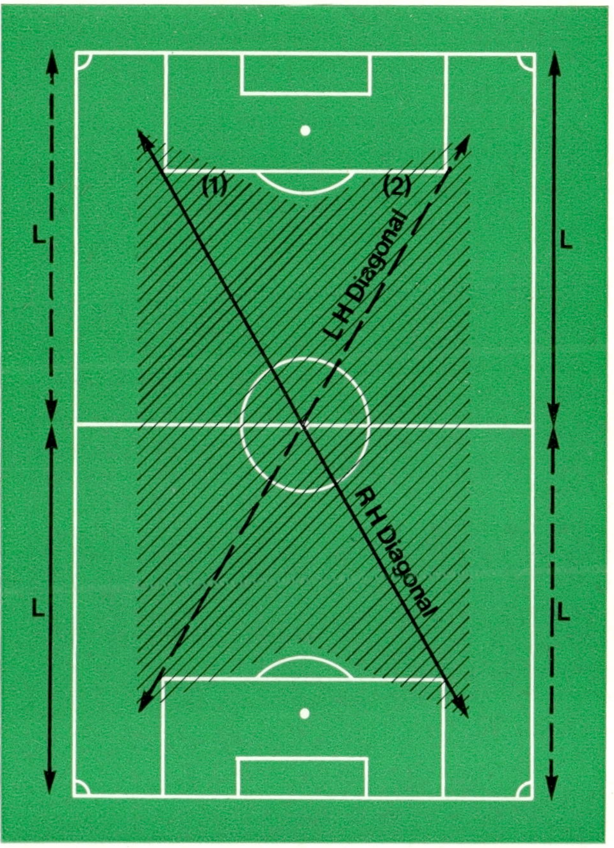

Questions on the Laws

(1) *When does a football match really start?*

(2) *When is a goal scored in Association Football?*

(3) *For what offences is a direct free kick awarded?*

(4) *State offences for which the punishment is an indirect free kick.*

(5) *Under what circumstances is a penalty kick retaken?*

(6) *The ball has been kicked into touch and before the throw-in is taken, a player deliberately kicks an opponent. The incident takes place in the penalty area of the former's side. What action should be taken by the referee and how should the game be restarted?*

(7) *A back standing a yard in front of his goal fists the ball to prevent a shot entering the net. However he merely deflects the ball into his goal. What is the decision?*

(8) *A referee is given certain powers in a match, but he has definite duties to perform. What are they?*

(9) *When is the ball out of play?*

(10) *If the following incidents occurred in a match in which you were the referee what would be your definite decision?*

(*a*) *Just as the goalkeeper is running to play the ball within his goal-area, an opponent charges him quite fairly.*

(*b*) *As the goalkeeper runs out to play a ball quite close to the penalty-spot, an attacker runs in, charges him fairly and gets possession.*

(*c*) *On a muddy ground, the goalkeeper takes a goal-kick. He miskicks and only sends the ball about 4 yards; so he runs forward, picks up the ball and punts it downfield.*

(*d*) *A wing-forward taking a throw-in quickly, has no colleague nearby so he throws it in properly, runs in and kicks it before anyone else can do so.*

(*e*) *Taking a penalty-kick, the kicker goes forward and back-heels the ball to a colleague who puts it past the goalkeeper.*

(*f*) *Taking a direct free kick just outside the opponent's penalty-area the kicker back-heels the ball to a colleague only 3 yards away and the ball goes into goal from the second player's shot.*

(*g*) *You order a penalty kick to be re-taken. Another player takes the second kick which scores.*

Answers

(1) The signal having been given by the referee, the ball is kicked into the opponents' half of the field for a distance of not less than 27 inches, from a still position and on the ground in the centre of the field of play, with all opponents at least 10 yards from the ball at the time it is kicked.

(2) When the whole of the ball has passed over the goal line, between the goal-posts and under the cross-bar, provided it has not been thrown, carried or propelled by hand or arm, by a player of the attacking side, except in the case of a goalkeeper, who is within his own penalty area.

(3) The nine penalty offences, viz.—Intentionally.

Hands and Arms
- Handling the ball
- Holding an opponent
- Striking or attempting to strike an opponent
- Pushing an opponent

Feet
- Tripping an opponent
- Kicking or attempting to kick an opponent
- Jumping at an opponent

Body
- Charging an opponent dangerously or violently
- Charging from behind an opponent who is not obstructing

(4) (a) Playing the ball a second time at the kick-off; a throw-in; a free kick; a penalty kick; a corner kick; free kick from within the penalty area or a goal kick when the ball has first passed beyond the penalty area.

(b) Interference with play in any way when in an offside position.

(c) Carrying by the goalkeeper

(d) Dangerous play.

(e) Charging a goalkeeper fairly within his own goal area, except when he is holding the ball or obstructing an opponent.

(f) Charging an opponent at the wrong time, the charge being otherwise fair.

(g) Intentionally obstructing an opponent when not attempting to play the ball.

(4) (h) Ungentlemanly conduct.

(j) Causing the game to be stopped.

(a) to caution a player for persistent infringement of the Laws or for dissenting, or

(b) to order off the field, a player persisting in misconduct after a caution or using foul or abusive language.

(5) (a) If a goal were scored and the attacking side infringed the Law.

(b) If a goal were *not* scored and the defending side committed the infringement.

(c) If the ball were stopped by an outside agent.

(6) Deal with the offender for deliberately kicking by a caution or by sending him off the field. Restart the game with a throw-in.

(7) A goal has been scored in accordance with the Law.

(8) (i) Enforce the Laws and decide disputed points.

(ii) Keep a record of the game and act as timekeeper.

(iii) Signal restarts.

(iv) Give permission for people to enter the field of play.

(v) Stop the game in case of serious injury, climatic or other interference.

(9) (i) When the whole of the ball has crossed the goal line or the touch line whether on the ground or in the air.

(ii) When the game has been stopped by the referee.

(10) (a) Award indirect free kick for infringement of Law 12 (2), 4.

(b) No offence, play continues.

(c) Order kick to be retaken — ball not in play until it has passed beyond penalty-area.

(d) Indirect free kick — player has played ball twice.

(e) Order kick to be retaken.

(f) Award a goal — opponents, not colleagues, must be 10 yards from ball.

(g) This is in order.

Schoolboy Football

SCHOOLBOY INTERNATIONAL FOOTBALL. The laws of the game are the same as given in the Referees' Chart with the following modifications:—

(1) *Playing Pitch:* Minimum size to be 80 yards by 60 yards.

(2) *Duration of Game:* Forty minutes each way. If weather is unfavourable 30 minutes each way may be played, subject to approval by the two Secretaries and Referee.

SENIOR SCHOOLBOY MATCHES. The English Schools' Football Association limits the time to 35 minutes each way. If weather is unfavourable 30 minutes each way may be played, subject to approval by the two Secretaries and Referee.

JUNIOR SCHOOLBOY MATCHES. (under 11 years of age). Modifications concerning conditions of play are left to the local organisations. Where circumstances permit a smaller minimum size of ground — 75/85 yards by 45/55 yards — and smaller goals — 7 yards wide by 6 feet 6 ins. high — are recommended.

It is also recommended that the penalty area should be reduced to two thirds of normal size, that a size 3 ball should be used and that the duration of such matches should not exceed 30 minutes each way.

The International Football Association Board

To bring about uniformity in the practice permitted on the field of play throughout the United Kingdom, an International Conference was held in December, 1882, to which each of the four British National Football Associations sent representatives. This Conference decided that only one set of Laws of the Game should apply wherever Association Football was played.

The result of this Conference was the establishment of the International Football Association Board which body alone was given the power to alter or amend the Laws of the Game. Since then no proposed alteration in Football Law is valid until it has been accepted by the Board whose decision thereon is at once binding on all Football Associations in membership. As the Federation International de Football Association is also a member of the Board, the laws as laid down operate throughout the world.

The laws have two main objects:—The control of the game and the protection of those who play. The laws apply equally to amateur and professional players, to senior and junior clubs, to friendly and competitive matches. There are but seventeen laws and they have evolved gradually as the outcome of more than one hundred years' playing experience.

It is impossible to legislate for every circumstance, imaginary as well as real, which might arise during the playing of a football match. Outside the strict letter of the law there may be incidents which can only be dealt with under the powers given to the referee to use his discretion.

The character of the game depends to a great extent upon the willing co-operation from those who play in complying with the laws and accepting the decisions of the referee.